# A Windy Day in Spring

by
Charles Ghigna

illustrated by
Laura Watson

PICTURE WINDOW BOOKS
a capstone imprint

Warm wind welcomes early spring.

Warm wind makes the bluebirds sing.

Warm wind rushes through the trees.

Warm wind stirs the bumblebees!

Warm wind blows a butterfly.

Warm wind lifts a kite up high.

Warm wind turns a weathervane.

Warm wind waves a pony's mane.

Warm wind makes the wind chimes ring.

Warm wind helps a hammock swing.

Warm wind steals a farmer's hat.

Warm wind pets a tabby cat!

Warm wind spins a blue pinwheel.

Warm wind makes a seagull squeal.

Warm wind pushes waves around.

Warm wind blows a castle down!

Warm wind fills a bright red sail.

Warm wind tickles a big blue whale.

Warm wind lifts an eagle's wings.

Warm wind does so many things!

# All About Wind

- Wind is the movement of air on Earth. Warm air rises, and cool air rushes in to replace it.
- People refer to wind by direction and speed. A weathervane tells us the direction of the wind. We measure wind speed with an anemometer.

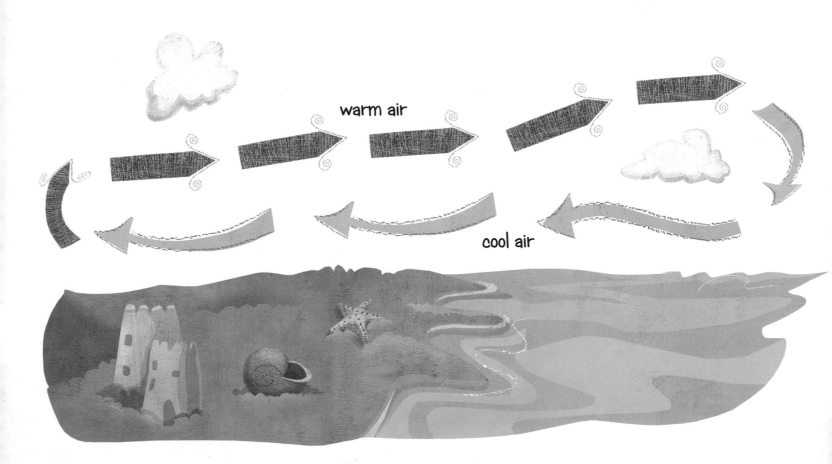

warm air

cool air

- A light wind is called a breeze. A gust is a quick, strong wind.
- Wind turbines create electricity with wind. Large blades on the turbine move when wind strikes them. The movement helps spin a generator. The generator creates electricity.

weathervane

wind turbine

anemometer

## All the Titles in This Set:

Hail to Spring!

Raindrops Fall All Around

Sunshine Brightens Springtime

A Windy Day in Spring

## Internet Sites

FactHound offers a safe, fun way to find Internet sites related to this book. All of the sites on FactHound have been researched by our staff.

Here's all you do:

Visit www.facthound.com

Type in this code: 9781479560325

Super-cool stuff!
Check out projects, games and lots more at
www.capstonekids.com

For Charlotte and Christopher.

Thanks to our adviser for his expertise, research, and advice:
Terry Flaherty, PhD, Professor of English
Minnesota State University, Mankato

Editors: Shelly Lyons and Elizabeth R. Johnson
Designer: Lori Bye
Art Director: Nathan Gassman
Production Specialist: Tori Abraham

The illustrations in this book were created with acrylics and digital collage.

Picture Window Books are published by Capstone,
1710 Roe Crest Drive, North Mankato, Minnesota 56003
www.capstonepub.com

Library of Congress Cataloging-in-Publication Data
Ghigna, Charles, author.
A windy day in spring / by Charles Ghigna ; illustrated by Laura Watson.
pages cm. — (Nonfiction picture books. Springtime weather wonders)
   Summary: "Introduces wind through fun, poetic text and colorful illustrations"—Provided by publisher.
   Audience: Ages 5-7.
   Audience: K to grade 3.
ISBN 978-1-4795-6032-5 (library binding : alk. paper)
ISBN 978-1-4795-6036-3 (big book)
ISBN 978-1-4795-6040-0 (ebook pdf)
ISBN 978-1-4795-6044-8 (board book)
1. Spring—Juvenile literature. 2. Winds—Juvenile literature. 3. Weather—Juvenile literature.
I. Watson, Laura, 1968- illustrator. II. Title.

Design Elements
Shutterstock: metrue

QB637.5.G486 2015
508.2—dc23                          2014029003

Printed in Canada.
092014    008478FRS15